OneNote Ultimate User Guide to Getting Things Done

Jack Ecko

Copyright © 2015 Jack Ecko

All rights reserved.

This document is geared towards providing exact and reliable information in regards to OneNote and Getting Things Done. The publication is sold with the agreement that the publisher is not providing accounting, officially permitted, or otherwise, qualified services. If advice is necessary, legal or professional, a practiced individual in the profession should be sought.

No part of this publication may be reproduced, duplicated, or transmitted in either electronic means or in printed format without the prior written permission of the publisher. Recording of this publication is strictly prohibited and any storage of this document is not allowed unless with written permission from the publisher. All rights reserved.

The information provided herein is stated to be truthful and consistent, in that any liability, in terms of inattention or otherwise, by any usage or abuse of any policies, processes, or directions contained within is the solitary and utter responsibility of the recipient reader. Under no circumstances will any legal responsibility or blame be held against the publisher for any reparation, damages, or monetary loss due to the information herein, either directly or indirectly.

Respective authors own all copyrights not held by the publisher.

The information herein is offered for informational purposes solely, and is universal as so. The presentation of the information is without contract or any type of guarantee assurance.

The trademarks that are used are without any consent, and the publication of the trademark is without permission or backing by the trademark owner. All trademarks and brands within this book are for clarifying purposes only and are owned by the owners themselves and not to be affiliated with this book.

CONTENTS

1	Getting the Introduction Done	1
2	Getting Things Done Productivity System (2015)	Pg 5
3	Is There Really Only One Note?	Pg 25
4	OneNote VS Evernote (Round1, Fight!)	Pg 27
5	Why OneNote?	Pg 33
6	Getting Down with OneNote	Pg 39
7	Setting up OneNote for GTD in 5 Savvy Steps	Pg 49
8	GTD & One Note in Tandem	Pg 67
9	6 Productivity Hacks & Tricks with OneNote	Pg 73
10	You've Won!	Pg 79
11	Free Bonus!	Pg 82
	More Resources	Pg 83

OneNote Ultimate User Guide to Getting Things Done

1 – GETTING THE INTRODUCTION DONE

Welcome to this book, which entails any and everything about Getting Things Done with OneNote!

If you've ever struggled to keep yourself organized…

Often start projects and never follow through with them…

Or find yourself consistently stressed about what needs to get done and can't decide on the next thing to do…

Then you've come to the right book. This guide provides you solutions to the issues experienced above as you will learn how to use one of (if not) the most popular organizational systems in the world, Getting Things Done, which has recently been revised in March 2015. Pairing this organizational system with one of the world's most popular digital note-taking software, OneNote, will help you overcome any productivity problems you may be experiencing and multiply your efficiency tenfold.

Throughout the book you'll learn how to keep on top of your workload, stay organized and, most importantly, GET THINGS

Getting the Introduction Done

DONE! All accomplished using one software, a world-class productivity system and an awesome book *ahem*!

As you progress through the book I highly, highly, HIGHLY recommend you take action on the steps outlined and practically apply the knowledge as you're reading through the book. While it's nice to read through the book in one go, it's even better to work your way through the steps outlined as you go through the book (not putting what you read into practice is like paying for an all you can eat buffet and not eating anything. You take a nice look around the buffet and gaze at all the mouth-watering food then turn around and leave the restaurant after paying – what the hell is the point!). By practically applying the concepts outlined you'll find it easier to learn how OneNote works, get your organizational system up and running and gain hands on experience with the GTD system.

You'll also gain an enormous sense of relief and be able to shake off A LOT of tension and stress (which some of you may unknowingly have!) once it's all up and running. By the end of it all you WILL be assured that you have setup a system that captures everything you need to know, do, organize and prioritize to easily get to where you want to go as quickly, seamlessly and as efficiently as possible.

Once you've read through the guide and put the steps into action, come back and use it as a reference whenever you feel the need to until the system becomes second nature for you and you know exactly what needs to get things done rapidly. If you struggle with parts of the software or how to use the GTD system then come back to the book and guide yourself through the specific areas that you're struggling with otherwise email me at techjackecko@gmail.com and I will happily respond.

Also please take note that although a complete system is presented here, it's MORE than acceptable, in fact, it's highly suggested that you adapt and modify the system to suit your needs or preferences. Whatever gets you working more productively is the end goal here and as it is in many cases, it's not one size fits all, so tweak and adapt the system for your unique needs and preferences.

> *"As to methods there may be a million and then some, but principles are few. The man who grasps principles can successfully select his own methods. The man who tries methods, ignoring principles, is sure to have trouble."*
>
> \- Ralph Waldo Emerson

You may be tempted to skip certain parts of the book if you're already familiar with Getting Things Done or OneNote – resist the urge! As we are linking OneNote to Getting Things Done and Getting Things Done to OneNote you may find a slightly different perspective on certain software features as well as certain parts of Getting Things Done. It's always good to refresh yourself on the main concepts of GTD as well to keep it fresh as you never know what you might pick up from things you missed on the first run through.

Getting the Introduction Done

This guide will cover the core concepts of the Getting Things Done system however please note that we will only be skimming the surface or going one layer deep into the overall arching system. It is highly recommended if you are not too familiar with the system to purchase David Allen's newly revised edition (http://amzn.to/1IFpNWs).

If you have previously read his older editions (like me), I still recommend giving the newer edition a read as it is a new experience and it never hurts to further familiarize yourself with something that works!

So, without any further ado – let's find out how you can start Getting Things Done!

2 - GETTING THINGS DONE PRODUCTIVITY SYSTEM (2015)

If you've never heard of Getting Things Done (GTD) before then you're in for a treat. GTD is a work-life management system devised by David Allen that was first published in 2001 under the same name. In March 2015, David Allen released a revised and updated version of his International Bestseller taking into account the rapid onset of technological advancements, cognitive scientific research and their implications on the GTD system and our productivity. I'll be covering some of these cognitive research studies later on.

The GTD system was developed to bring order to chaos so that you can achieve stress-free productivity. You can think of the GTD system much like highway codes and road names, the only twist here is to apply the same concept to organizational skills. Without highway codes or road names, cars would drive in all sorts of directions and nobody would ever get anywhere or if you do manage to finally get somewhere it definitely wasn't the most efficient route possible - the same thing is most likely occurring in your life if you don't have a productivity system in place!

Most people find they're incredibly busy, and it's no wonder with so many things vying for our attention (have you noticed the substantial amount of billboards, TV ads and online pop up ads with companies basically jumping in front of your face shouting "pick me, pick me, pick me!").

It's no surprise that being able to stay organized in this world is incredibly difficult – just think about the stacks or piles of paper you have scattered around your work space or office, as well as the many things you have bouncing around in your head at this single moment in time… Things that you have to-do, people you have to get back to and urgent reminders you have to juggle inside of your head so you don't forget to complete them.

One of the main goals and priorities of the GTD system is to get EVERYTHING you need to do out of your head so that you can operate with a "mind like water" thus allowing you to easily enter into the "zone" or flow state where things are done seamlessly and almost effortlessly. This concept first derived from athletes that would enter into a state termed "flow" during their performances. Athletes would often find they were no longer consciously performing yet everything would flow smoothly and effortlessly. This concept is detailed thoroughly in *Flow* by Mihaly Csikszentmihalyi and more recently a practical application of the concept has been detailed in Stephen Kotler's, *The Rise of Superman: Decoding the Science of Ultimate Human Performance*. The underlying principle here is to not be a human doing that is constantly thinking about the things you need to do, but rather to be a human BEING that does the things you ought to be doing in the present moment without niggling thoughts running around in your mind.

The idea of having a "mind like water" derives from karate, where you're required to clear your mind and relax in order to achieve the appropriate levels of strength and power for optimal efficiency (**Fun fact:** David Allen is a Karate black belt). If you ever find yourself operating from a tense and anxious state, you'll notice that in retrospect operating from this state narrows your perspective and impairs your ability to accomplish tasks efficiently. This is the same for karate and other sports, when your muscles are too tense you operate with less flexibility, range of motion and ability to perform at your greatest potential. People who don't have a "mind like water" often respond inappropriately to situations because they are controlled by situations which cause them to underreact or overreact given the context of the situation. As you can imagine, responding inappropriately to situations leads to suboptimal results.

Our brains were not made to function as storage spaces, they were made to think creatively and find solutions to problems. It's been found that having to store things diminishes our clarity and focus and hence our productivity. In the 2008 research paper *Getting Things Done: The Science Behind Stress-Free Productivity* written by two researchers from Belgium who analyzed the GTD methodology, the researchers came to the profound conclusion that your mind is designed to have ideas based upon pattern recognition, but it isn't designed to remember much of anything. This is due to the way the mind developed in prehistoric times and as a result our minds are brilliant at recognition, but terrible at recall.

This finding is further supported in Daniel Levitin's *The Organized Mind* which emphasizes that when you use your memory as your organizing system, your mind will effectively become overwhelmed and incompetent as it is working at a higher intensity level due to performing work it's not suited for. Another interesting cognitive science conclusion brought to light by Dr Roy Baumeister is that the completion of uncompleted tasks does not relieve the burden on the psyche of having to remember these uncompleted tasks. What is needed is a trusted plan that ensures forward engagement will happen which is in essence the core of the GTD system.

Once you have the GTD system in place you will have a fool proof system for keeping track of the things you need to do, should do or are *thinking about* doing and this provides you with mental clarity and space for you to focus on the things that matter and enhance your likelihood of entering "flow" or having a "mind like water" as you undertake your work.

"The art of resting the mind and the power of dismissing from it all care and worry is probably one of the secrets of our great men"

– Captain J. A. Hatfield

The three key objectives of the GTD system are to:

1. Capture all the things that might need to get done or have usefulness for you – now, later, someday, big, little, or in between – in a logical and trusted system outside your head and off your mind

2. Directing yourself to make front-end decisions about all of the "inputs" you let into your life so that you will always have a workable inventory of "next actions" that you can implement or renegotiate in the moment

3. Curating and coordinating all of the content, utilizing the recognition of the multiple levels of commitments with yourself and others that you have at play, at any single point in time.

To begin with, we will discuss the context of the lists that are used in the GTD system which we will learn how to set up in OneNote in Chapter 7. The contexts of these lists are provided first so you can gain an understanding of them before we start implementing them, from this understanding you gain an idea of why and what these lists are used for:

The "In" (or Capture) List

This list will hold and capture all your ideas or tasks as they come to you (literally or figuratively), for example, if your boss asks you get his suit dry cleaned you'll put this into your "in" list or if you remember that you've scheduled a coffee catchup with Mike but forgot to note it down in your calendar – you'll put these ideas or tasks into your "in" list. These items/ideas/tasks are all considered to be "open loops" – anything that does not belong where it is, the way it is will pull on your attention if it's not appropriately managed and as such are open loops until they are complete or finished.

If this is your first time implementing an organizational system you'll want to set aside time the near future (at least 2 hours - some people have taken up to 6 hours and longer to do this) and write down ALL, yes, I do mean ALL of the different things that currently aren't the way you want them to be. This includes things you will need to do, to things you've been meaning to do.

This may seem like a daunting task at first but trust me, it's worth it and is a lot easier to do then you would expect (and quite fun as well once you get into the groove of it).

After the initial set up and processing of your "in" list (which we get into later), this list serves as the list that captures everything that comes to you. From here, the ideas or tasks on your "in" list will be processed once a day, or every other day. This process is the backbone of the GTD system and will enable you to enhance your efficiency and streamline your actions.

How to Process Your "In" List in 3 Steps

After you've written down all the possible tasks that you could think of, you'll go through each item on your "in" list one at a time. It's important that you go through the list in the order in which you wrote them down so you don't get lost or confused and more importantly, so you don't place higher importance on an item which may eventually sidetrack you from doing the task at hand - which is to process your "in" list. Once you have the item from your "in" list in front of you, you need to ask yourself a series of questions.

1. **"Is it actionable?"**

This question is asked so that you can determine if you're able to perform a clear, physical and specific action that will achieve the outcome desired. If the answer is no, you either get rid of it (delete it), move it to your reference list, or put it into a someday/maybe list (both lists will be discussed later).

2. **If the answer is yes, then you need to ask "What is the next action?"**

This action needs to be something you can actually perform; it needs to be a physical and visible action. For example: make a call, type up the report or sign off on the award agreement. Don't specify an action which is vague such as "plan for the competition" make it clear and specific such as "email Dave for the competition entry price." It's always better to be clear and specific when it comes to next actions.

By spending time coming up with a physical AND visible action you will make sure that your 'Next Actions' list is filled with ACTIONABLE items that you can pick up and do at any time. This increases the likelihood that you'll accomplish the actions significantly as you know exactly what you need to do, and all you are required to do is just do it! Without a next action, there remains a potentially infinite gap between the current reality and what you need to do to accomplish the intended outcome. The best way to close this gap is to write down the very next physical action required that will move the current situation forward. If you had nothing else to do in your life but get closure on this, what visible action would you take right now? Once you have defined the specific next action move on to…

3. **Asking yourself, "Will this action take less than 2 minutes to complete?"**

If the answer is yes – drop everything and do it straight away!

If the answer is no, you either delegate it to someone more appropriate to undertake the action. You can do this by writing down who you've delegated the task to and making a note of this in your waiting for list, otherwise you will defer the next action by putting it into the 'Next Actions' list.

The 2 minute rule depends on your own circumstances and time available, if you're short on time to process your "in" list, you can lower it to 30 seconds. If you have more time then you can increase it to 5 or 10 minutes.

Remember triple D when it comes to processing your "in" list and you won't go wrong: Do it, Delegate it or Defer it.

You can only feel good about what you're not doing when you know everything you're not doing.

Three Reasons Things Are on Your Mind

Remember, most often the reason that something is on your mind is because you want something to be different than what it currently is and you haven't:

1. Clarified exactly what the outcome is;
2. Decided what the very next physical action step is to change it; or
3. Put reminders of the outcome and the action required in a system you trust.

Any "would, could, or should" commitment held only in the psyche creates irrational and unresolvable pressure, 24-7.

This is why the "Next Actions" list is so powerful at moving us forward...

"Next Actions" List

This is a list of your... well... next actions, believe it or not! This is the list you will refer to once you've finished a task you were previously working on or require a new task to start working on. From here, you'll determine the next action to complete off this list based on what's most appropriate for the given context, time, energy and focus you have available. Rinse and repeat this process and you become a productivity machine!

A quick tip for determining when the next action is done comes down to two basic components that are required:

1. Defining what done means (the outcome); and
2. What doing looks like (the specific, physical action).

You will most likely end up with 25-150+ next actions depending on how many items you initially captured in your in list. The more next actions you have, the better it is to build sub-lists within your next actions list which will be broken down by contexts (refer to below) that separate your next actions and divides them into more manageable groups.

There is usually an inverse relationship between how much something is on your mind and how much it's getting done.

"Waiting For" List

This is a list of things which you're waiting for someone else to complete. This list can comprise a number of things, mainly it will be for work you've delegated to someone else, an email you're waiting on a reply to or work that requires input from someone else before it can be completed.

The most important part of this list is that you review it weekly or as often as you need to so that these actions you've delegated aren't running around rampant in your mind. A great tip for this list is to ensure you note down the date at which the action was delegated to the appropriate person AND write down when you expect the action to be completed by. This makes it easier when you need to chase people up in the near future.

Projects List

Projects are defined as an outcome which requires more than one action step to achieve the intended outcome within a years' time. This book is an example of a project because its outcome is to provide valuable information on OneNote and GTD. To accomplish this outcome a number of actions must be done before it can be achieved such as writing the chapters, editing the book, formatting it correctly and proofreading the text. Always ensure that you have at least one project task in your "next actions" list so you don't forget about your projects!

This project list puts a stake in the ground so that you're reminded of the open loop which is the project and the loop is only closed once your outcomes are achieved. A weekly review of this list is a MUST and will bring these outcomes back to you as something that's still outstanding. The projects list ensures they stay fresh and alive in your management system (versus your head) until it is completed or eliminated. The definition of a project means some rather small things you may not normally consider projects are going to be present on this list, as well as some bigger ones you would normally consider a project.

The Projects list is not meant to hold all the plans or details about your projects, and it doesn't matter if the projects are prioritized by size or urgency. This list simply serves as a comprehensive index of your open loops. You won't be working off your projects list, it's simply used as a placeholder during the weekly review to ensure you have next action steps defined for all your projects during the review and that nothing is falling through the cracks.

Note: You don't actually do a project; you can only do action steps related to it.

Examples of projects include:

- Take a Spring holiday
- Publish book
- File tax returns
- Renovate kitchen
- Get a new editor on board

- Research resources for video project

"Someday/Maybe" list

This is a list of things that you want to do, experience or accomplish in the near future. The reason you might want to wait to do these things could vary - it could be due to needing more time to do it properly or it could be something you want to do however you need more expertise on the subject matter so you are required to set aside time for research before you can get started. This list is present because you'd like to be reminded of the possibility of accomplishing these things in the near future.

Trigger List

This is a list of trigger words to get your mind going in the right direction in case you have any ideas or actions that you need to do that are still bouncing around in your head. These trigger words could be things like 'boss', 'projects not completed' or 'projects to start' which may reveal something that has been hiding in the corner of your mind that you had forgotten about. If anything does pop up on review of your trigger list, you should know what to do by now – put it into your "in" list!

Trigger word examples:

Professional

Projects started, not completed

Projects that need to be started

"Look into.. projects

Commitments/promises to others

Boss/partners

Colleagues

Subordinates

Others in organization

Financial

Cash

Budgets

Forecasts

Balance Sheet

Banks

Credit Line

Personal

Projects started, not completed

Projects that need to be started

Projects in service

Community

Volunteer

Spiritual organization

Commitments/promises to others

Cooking

Health

Sports

I highly recommend that you modify these words to add your own words that will help you identify and capture those wandering thoughts.

Contexts

These are tags you will use to break down your "Next Actions" list; these tags remind you of what is necessary to accomplish the action tagged. For example if your next action is to write up a sales report for the last month you'll most likely require a computer to type up the sales figures from last month, or you may need a phone to make calls to pay outstanding invoices.

Next to the actions, you would type out the 'context' you'd need to complete it and put a @ sign in front of it. So the context would be @computer or @phone, this helps immensely when you find yourself in different work environments or during waiting periods where you could be getting things done instead of staring off into space. I will cover a nifty trick we can use in OneNote to create contexts more efficiently for next actions once we begin setting up the GTD system.

Calendar

You **MUST** only use your calendar to record actions that must be done by a certain date. If you only think you would like to have things done by a certain date, leave them off your calendar. This way, your calendar is only filled with items that **MUST** be done and this makes it much easier to keep track of your MUSTS and ENSURES that these tasks are completed on the dates they must be completed by instead of having your calendar inundated with should and coulds (which is what your next action list is for!).

If your calendar gets cluttered with events or tasks that may or may not need to be done, it makes it tremendously difficult to distinguish your MUSTS from your COULDS or SHOULDS and your MUSTS can get lost in the crowd easily which results in a higher likelihood of them not getting done.

Your Next Actions lists, along with your calendar are at the heart of daily action management organization and orientation. Your calendar will determine the core of your day as you complete your musts and once they've been completed your next action lists will be worked on.

Reference List

Many things that come your way will require no action, however it will hold intrinsic value in the information that it provides. These items are things you'll want to keep on hand and be able to retrieve as needed.

These include anything from the online menu to local restaurants, list of internet resources you don't often frequent enough to warrant a bookmark however would like to keep at hand or a list of restaurants you like to frequent and could be used to decide on a restaurant for the night. Further examples include: manuals for software, local takeout deli menu, kid's sports team schedule, list of internal phone extensions and the list goes on.

Weekly Review

You will want to perform a review of everything once a week (I suggest you set aside some time on a Friday, Saturday or Sunday for this). Friday would be the best time in the early afternoon if you work a normal weekday job as outstanding work will be fresh in your mind and you'll be able to delegate work and wrap up the work week nicely to enjoy your weekend that isn't spent mulling over what needs to get done on Monday. Set aside at least 30 minutes to review your lists and your calendar to check everything is in order and to measure how you're progressing along with your projects.

Review your projects and ensure that each one has at least a corresponding "Next Action" listed in your next actions list. You will also want to double check that all of your "Next Actions" are actionable items or things you can physically do – if they aren't, either edit them to be more specific or put them in the someday/maybe or reference list, otherwise trash it. Make sure that actions which have been completed are archived or deleted so your lists don't get cluttered.

Look through your someday/maybe list and evaluate the reasons why these items were put on the list in the first place. You want to quickly determine if these reasons are still applicable. If they are no longer applicable and there is something you can now work on for these items - move them over onto the projects/next actions list.

Review your "waiting for" list and take the time to get in touch with anyone that you need an update from.

Last but not least, you'll want to skim through your "trigger list" at the end of your review to see if anything is still bouncing around in your head which you haven't listed down yet for your "in" list.

Phew, that was quite a bit to absorb but have no fear - we'll be covering this material again later on in the book when we're setting the system up and as always you are welcome to refer back to this section anytime.

The key takeaways and the main goal of the weekly review are to take the time to:

1. Gather and process all your stuff.

2. Review your system.

3. Update your lists.

4. Get clean, clear, current, and complete on your projects and lists

Review whatever lists, overviews, and orientation maps you need to, as often as you need to, to get their contents off your mind.

Now that we've gone through the basic structure of GTD and how it works we'll move on to the tool that we'll be using to GET THINGS DONE - Microsoft OneNote!

3 - IS THERE REALLY ONLY ONE NOTE?

So, what the heck is OneNote?!

OneNote is a free software tool developed by Microsoft which serves as a digital note-taker. It has the ability to gather notes, drawings, screen captures, audio clips and is widely available on desktops, laptops, mobiles and tablets.

First released in 2003, a multitude of features are offered on OneNote such as the ability to write notes that are accessible from multiple devices as your notes are synced to the OneDrive cloud storage. This provides you the ability to type up a note at home on your desktop, pick it up while you're on the train with your mobile and edit it once you reach the office.

OneNote is similar to Evernote (another popular digital note-taking software) as both provide similar note taking and search abilities, in addition however, OneNote offers added integration with Microsoft Office. With OneNote you're able to link notes you've taken to PowerPoint, Excel and Word which serves to be highly useful (and has been a lifesaver for me on many occasions!) depending on your occupation. If you need to create documents or spreadsheets from your notes then OneNote also has the ability to do so. The differences between OneNote and Evernote have been done to death over the years and I summarize and highlight the major differences in the following chapter.

Another great feature of OneNote is that it's possible to easily move your notes into an email with Outlook providing you the ability to quickly share notes with others in a few clicks. OneNote also shares the ability to allow you to work together with others by sharing notes so that they are able to view, edit and add to them. Being able to share your notes helps turn a simple piece of note-taking software into a brilliant open workspace resulting in the production of mastermind ideas (google "whiteboarding onenote" for more).

The search option within OneNote allows you to easily find notes you need, even if the words you're looking for are in images taken from screen captures, scanned documents or audio clips! This means you can quickly and easily pull up a scanned document in your notes, which is more efficient than individually going through each of your filed documents looking for the correct document.

Wrapped up in a nutshell, OneNote is not just a note-taker, but it's also a wonderful productivity tool with a ton of nifty shortcuts, tips and tricks that come along with it. By linking an amazingly powerful tool like OneNote with the GTD system your productivity will no doubt benefit.

4 - ONENOTE VS EVERNOTE (ROUND 1 - FIGHT!)

Of course in today's advanced technological age there's more than one note-taking software package on the market and you may be wondering why OneNote should be chosen above the rest. Well, seeing as the most popular note-taking software packages on the market today are OneNote and Evernote a comparison is provided here to give you a rundown of the pros and cons of each.

If you've never used either of these software packages before then it's worth taking a look at both of them before determining which one to pull the trigger on, so let's compare the pair so that you know you're using the best one suited for your needs.

What is Evernote?

Evernote is a popular software package which provides you the ability to take notes and access them over a number of different platforms. It's a "freemium" software package meaning it's available to download for free – but you will need to pay extra if you want to use the premium features of it.

A free account allows you to use Evernote on any device, but you won't be able to access files offline whilst on Android or iOS. You are also provided with less storage space on a free account which is understandable.

Evernote originally launched in 2008 in an open beta test on Windows, Mac and mobile devices and the popularity of Evernote grew so rapidly such that by 2011 it had reached a user base of 11 million people.

Today, Evernote is available on Windows, OS X, Chrome OS, Android, Blackberry, iOS, Windows Mobile and Windows Phones. If you make a note on one device you can easily pick it up and edit it on any other device using the software.

Which Is Better at Keeping Notes?

Both OneNote and Evernote mimic a system for keeping notes, letting you take down notes quickly and easily while storing them so that you don't have to carry a notepad and pen with you everywhere.

Both offer very similar features, such as text recognition for images, the ability to store notes online and cross-integrate between devices, however, the approach that each one takes for these features differ slightly.

OneNote's user interface is laid out as close to a physical

notebook as you could possibly imagine on a digital platform. You're given the ability to setup more than one notebook if required and with each notebook, you can create separate sections and individual pages under each of these sections. One of the greatest benefits of OneNote is the speed at which you can take notes wherever you are with the added ability to format your notes just as easily as you can on Microsoft Word with bullet points, numbered lists and formatted styles. OneNote is effective for taking down notes in multiple formats such as lists, mind maps or brainstorming sessions as you have the ability to move text, images or drawings around the page easily much like a physical notebook.

Evernote uses a no-frills interface which is more conducive to taking down simple notes, rather than stylized ones. Evernote is at its best when it comes to storing your notes for easy retrieval later on, for this reason it's generally used as a "digital filing cabinet." A really useful feature of Evernote is that you're able to use Google searches to go through your notes and as such serves a very useful way of retrieving them later on, hence why it's generally used as a digital filing cabinet.

Evernote is slightly better when it comes to storing notes for easy retrieval later on, especially when it pertains to large amounts. However, as a digital notebook, OneNote is by far the better of the two if you want your notes to be organized efficiently. Not only is it possible to take down notes quickly but you also have the features available to edit your notes into a quality document later on if necessary. Think of Evernote as a waiter's pad where you can easily and quickly write down notes whereas OneNote serves as a proper notebook or journal with different sections and pages for better organization.

Which Has Better Integration?

Both OneNote and Evernote are able to integrate with other software packages, however the ease of integration and cross-compatibility varies between the two programs.

As you can imagine, OneNote is able to link with other Microsoft products with ease and more efficiency than Evernote can. OneNote has a large amount of shortcuts available that can be used on your desktop or laptop even if OneNote isn't open. OneNote also has the ability to integrate with Word, Excel and Outlook to provide greater functionality. The features you can use with Outlook – adding reminders, emailing notes and sending meeting details to OneNote – make it a great tool for your work-life. You can also add additional features from installing third party add-ons; the number of third party add-ons available at this current moment of time is small but the market has been gaining traction in recent times and I find personally that the features offered by OneNote are more than enough for current needs.

Evernote can integrate with Microsoft software, but not as easily or effectively as OneNote. Evernote's strengths lie in its ability to link with third party apps as it was made with the intention of third party integration from day one. There are many add-ons you can download and use in conjunction with Evernote to enhance your productivity.

OneNote wins hands down for its integration with Windows and obviously this comes with an unfair advantage – but it is incredibly useful to anyone who uses Windows for work. Evernote has an advantage over OneNote with third party add-ons, but the gap is closing rapidly.

Which Works Better on Mobile?

Both OneNote and Evernote have a mobile app which is accessible from smartphones and tablets. Of course, sometimes desktop apps don't always make the transition to mobile too well, which has the upper hand here?

Despite being incredibly easy to use on mobile, OneNote's mobile app is not as feature-rich as the desktop version. It seems as though the makers of the app decided to only include features they thought mobile users would need, rather than throwing everything in that they thought they would like. You can add notes, read notes, move notes around and pin notes to the home screen – but advanced features beyond this aren't available in the app.

Evernote is a more feature-rich mobile app than OneNote is. It appears as though the developers worked to ensure all of the features were available on mobile and tweaked them well enough to make their mobile experience as user friendly as their desktop application. Including the usual features offered by OneNote on mobile, Evernote also allows you to switch notes to other notebooks, share them and set reminders on notes.

Evernote gains an advantage over OneNote here by providing a much greater and more feature rich mobile experience. Both note-taking software make the transition to mobile use with incredible ease, but OneNote is let down by only bringing over some of the features available from the desktop version.

Summary

Choosing between OneNote and Evernote can be an incredibly tough choice or an utterly simple choice based on your requirements and needs for a note-taking software. Evernote is better for mobile use, storage and third party integration, whereas OneNote is better for note-taking, stylized editing and integration with Windows.

In the end, thanks to the integration with Microsoft software alongside the note-taking and editing benefits offered by OneNote, I would highly recommend using OneNote out of the two apps.

Personally I use OneNote as my digital-note taking app and sporadically use Evernote for large lists when I'm doing some serious brainstorming or idea generation. The other determining factor to consider between the two is where you spend the majority of your time at work, on a computer or on a mobile?

I'd make a sure bet that the majority of you spend more than 60% of your working time on the computer as opposed to your mobile.

5 - WHY ONENOTE?

It isn't difficult to see how useful OneNote could be for the GTD system. By utilizing the powerful note taking features of the software, especially the note book layout, we can turn OneNote into a monstrous productivity tool. Below are the top reasons why using OneNote for GTD is optimal.

Manage Tasks Wherever You Are

OneNote is available on practically any device you own, this means that you will be able take down new tasks or thoughts anytime and anywhere. If you get a call from your boss at 2 in the morning while you're holidaying in the Bahamas (after you've held back the urge to scream at him for waking you up) you can add the task he's assigned to you into your "in" list by using your mobile.

You can also manage your lists wherever you happen to find yourself. If your laptop runs out of charge or you're working somewhere you aren't able to use your desktop, you can still load up your next actions list and immediately make progress on a task which doesn't require a laptop or desktop (and this is quickly determined from the contexts you've set for your actions!). You can also easily perform reviews for your lists, even if you don't have the device you usually use (or physical folders) on hand. This increases your productivity immensely. Instead of having to put off a review in circumstances where doing work simply isn't convenient, such as travelling on a busy train you'll be able to refer to your mobile and lists from there and do it on the go. Whatever the reasons are, the flexibility of being able to add, manage, and review your lists on the go will aid tremendously in your productivity.

Delegate with Ease

By integrating OneNote with Outlook you have the fun ability to delegate your workload in a few simple clicks. You can work through your Next Actions list and send off an e-mail to the person you've delegated the task to along with the notes they need to get started, and you can also update your notes to remind yourself of who's been delegated the task and when the it's due.

Being able to delegate tasks in this way makes things a lot easier for you and the person being delegated the task. You don't need to re-type an email to cover all the points you've made in your notes, and you don't need to make a lengthy phone call or invite the person into your office to explain everything to them. You simply send them an e-mail with your notes, make a quick phone call and tell them you've sent them an e-mail (optional) and that you'll be available for any questions they might have after they've gone through the notes. This means you'll only need to take time out and explain the finer details if the other person is genuinely struggling with the work you've delegated them and the person won't be interrupted in the middle of whatever they're doing disrupting their flow.

Simple Layout

OneNote's layout is perfect for getting things done. You can set up as many notebooks for GTD as you need. For example you might want to separate your home life and work life and this could mean creating a notebook for work and one for home. Or alternatively, keep separate lists under one notebook to separate the two out.

You can set up sections or sections groups for your different lists and the page system makes it easy to manage all your notes on a separate page. Thanks to this simple layout, which lends itself to GTD perfectly, you won't need to fiddle around finding the right folder for all your notes as it will be laid out aesthetically for your ease of use.

Screen Capturing

One of the great features in OneNote is the option to screen capture or take photos directly into your notes. This feature will often make it a lot easier to capture tasks as opposed to copying and pasting all of the details you require over into OneNote.

This screen capturing ability isn't limited to just the mobile; you'll also have the ability to capture screen clippings from your desktop by pressing "Windows Key (next to Ctrl and Alt) + S" activating the screen clipping feature allowing you to simply drag your mouse over the area you would like to capture. After you have selected the area, OneNote will ask you where you would like the screen clipping to be placed.

This can be highly useful if you need to save any online research articles or lengthy texts into your notes – pairing this feature with OneNote's ability to copy the text from images saves an exorbitant amount of time.

An added bonus thanks to the powerful search options in OneNote means you'll be able to search the text in the pictures or images that you've taken, which is useful if you ever need to bring up a note quickly.

Quick and Easy Processing

Processing everything that's in your "in" list can be a chore sometimes. It can be frustrating having to copy and paste all of the information between the lists, or having to take things out of one folder and placing them into another folder.

Using OneNote makes this a much, much easier and more

enjoyable process to get through. In OneNote all you have to do is right click the note or use the plethora of keyboard shortcuts to move your notes straight in to the folder that it needs to go in.

6 - GETTING DOWN WITH ONENOTE

Before we integrate GTD with OneNote it's important you first set up and gain familiarity with using OneNote. The three most commonly used features of OneNote for GTD are laid out below and we suggest as you read through this chapter that you utilize the features and play around with them to get familiarized.

Setting up OneNote

The first thing you will need to do is download OneNote onto your devices (www.onenote.com). OneNote is available on the following operating systems: Microsoft Windows, OS X, iOS, Android, Symbian, Windows Mobile and Windows Phone so all your devices should essentially be covered!

You'll want to download OneNote onto all available devices as this ensures it will be accessible at any given moment in time allowing you to pick up or take down notes wherever and whenever you're required to.

The only requirement for OneNote is a Microsoft account which is available for free. If you have a Hotmail, Live or Outlook e-mail account then you already have a Microsoft account and you can use these accounts to login if you wish. If you don't have one, you can sign up for a new Microsoft account using a Gmail, Outlook.com or Yahoo address (your email doesn't have to be Microsoft based).

Go ahead, sign up and download OneNote, it may take some time to set up but that's okay, I'll be here gladly waiting!

Once you've finished downloading OneNote and you've signed in using your Microsoft account, let's get to it! Please note that its best practice to use OneNote when your devices are connected to the internet as this will allow notes to be synced to OneDrive (the internet cloud storage for your notes) which provides you the ability to access your most up to date notes on all devices.

The issue with working offline on OneNote is that you may end up with conflicting pages. It's possible that as you change notes on separate devices, the updates won't be uploaded to OneDrive until your devices are connected to the internet and as a result different versions will be uploaded creating a conflict. It's more than okay to work offline on one device for an extended period of time, you must ensure however that once you're back online all your notes have synced up to the latest version before you try editing them from another device.

The OneNote Layout

The design of OneNote mimics a real note book with the design layout split into notebooks, sections and pages. The toolbar at the top provides most of the tools which are available in Microsoft Word allowing you to change the font and styles of texts as well as contexts or checklists for notes in your lists.

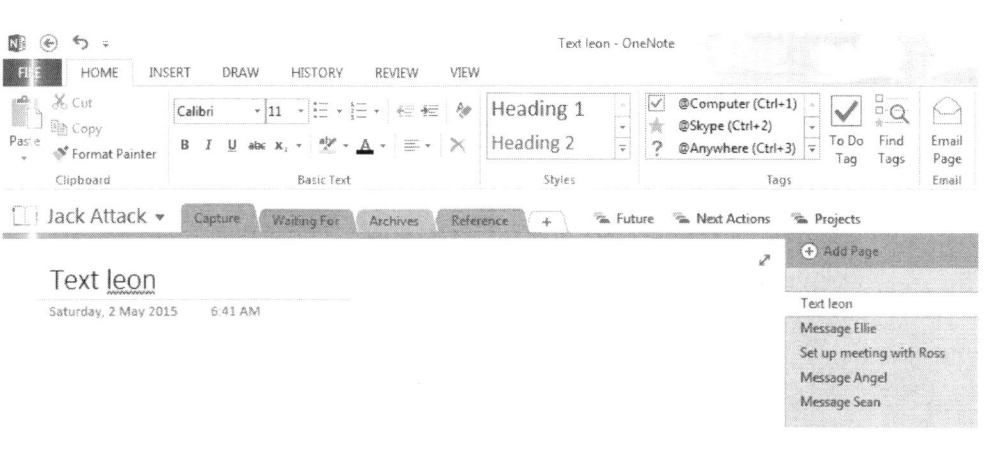

When you start OneNote up for the first time, your notebooks will be shown on the right window pane. You can set up as many notebooks as you like by clicking on the "File" tab at the top of the toolbar (this will only appear if you are currently in a notebook), otherwise if you're already in the "File" tab (shown in the diagram below) then click on "New" displayed in the options on the left.

Ensure you select "OneDrive – Personal" then type in your new notebook name and "Create Notebook". You want to make sure you select OneDrive so your notes are stored into the online cloud which will allow your notes to be readily available on all your devices.

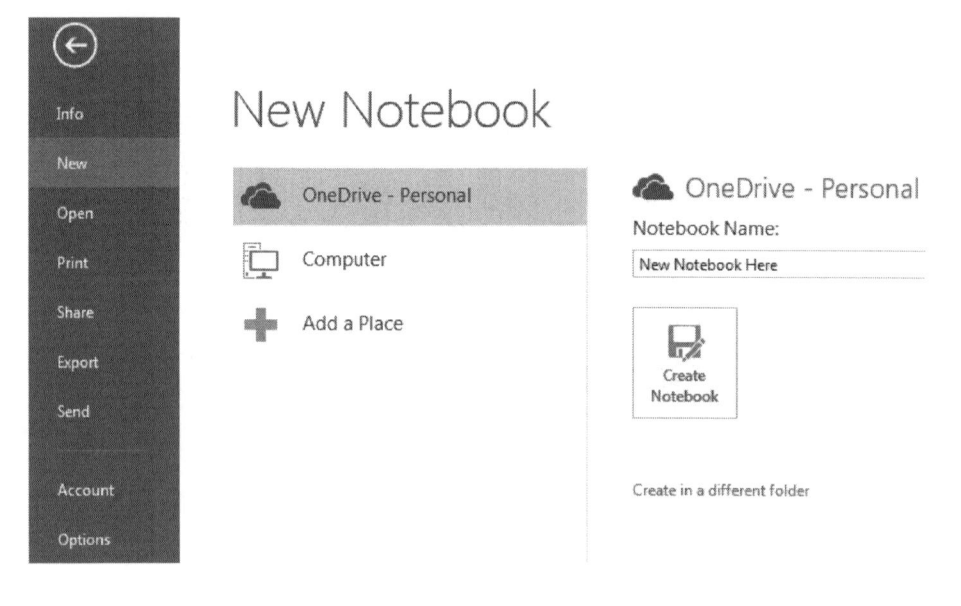

In each notebook you will have sections that hold your notes; these sections are shown at the top of the note book as clickable tabs (see the below tabs for 'Capture', 'Waiting For', 'Archives' and 'Reference' which are the sections).

You can set up a new section by right-clicking on the row of tabs and clicking "New Section" (Ctrl + T for shortcut) or "New Section Group". A new section group provides you the ability to create further sections under the titled section group. For instance, "Future", "Next Actions" and "Projects" are all section groups, when you click into them it's essentially a new notebook where you can have further sections listed. So for "Projects" you could house new sections for each of your projects that are separated out for each area of your life (i.e. family, work, health etc).

The pages you have under a section are listed on the right hand side of the notebook. You can label the pages so that you know exactly what's held within each page. To add pages/notes to your sections/lists click on "New Page" (or Ctrl + N).

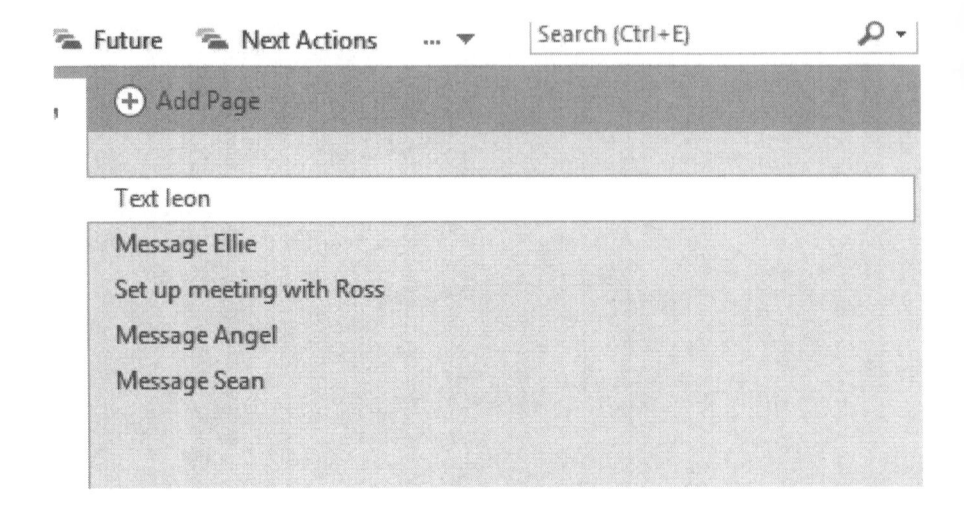

| Future | Next Actions | ... ▼ | Search (Ctrl+E) | 🔎 ▼ |

⊕ Add Page

Text leon
Message Ellie
Set up meeting with Ross
Message Angel
Message Sean

Taking Notes

To take notes on OneNote all you have to do is click anywhere on the blank page and start typing your notes out, paste images or files. These notes can then be easily organized by moving the text boxes or images around the page to arrange your notes in an order that you visually prefer. This maneuverability makes it easy to prioritize your notes in an order of importance or group them into related clusters.

Brainstorm
Saturday, 2 May 2015   8:31 AM

```
            I'm hilarious

         Why I'm so awesome

I'm good looking         I wear glasses
```

At first glance OneNote might seem basic in design but this is because the editing tools are hidden by default to resemble a real note book. If you click on a tab at the top of the page (Home, Insert, Draw, History, Review or View) the extra options will then reveal themselves. You can keep these options visible at all times by double clicking on any of the tabs - you can hide them by doing the same.

As well as typing out notes, you have the ability to add pictures or files to your notes with the "Insert" tab. If you're using a computer you can add screen clippings by using the keyboard shortcut **Windows + S** and then clicking and dragging your mouse over the area of the screen you want capture as previously discussed. You can also record video and audio notes by clicking on the relevant option under the "Insert" tab in OneNote granted you have the correct accessories to record video and audio clips.

Searching Notes

As mentioned in the last chapter, it's possible to search for text in any of your notes – including your images! All you need to do is tap on the search box in the top right hand corner of the screen (or Ctrl + E for the shortcut) and type out what you want to search for.

OneNote utilizes an incredibly powerful search algorithm so that you can quickly search through your notes to find anything you might need. A common crux that I find with this feature however is that some people tend to rely on this tool too much, and as a result end up with a bucket load of disjointed notes which aren't organized properly into sections and pages. Relying solely on searching for notes in this manner is a suboptimal way of properly storing and organizing your notes so I highly suggest you do not substitute the search bar for proper organization!

	project	×
Finished: All Notebooks (change)	Find on page (Ctrl+F)	

Recent picks
- 📁 Projects — (Jack Attack)

In title: project (1)
- 📄 3 projects — (Jack Attack> Projects> Kindl...

On page: project (4)
- 📄 2 — (Jack Attack> Projects> Kindl...
- 📄 Part 1 — (Jack Attack> Projects> Kindl...
- 📄 7 — (Jack Attack> Projects> Kindl...
- 📄 5 Capturing — (Jack Attack> Projects> Kindl...

Recycle Bins (2)
- 🗑 Projects — (Jack Attack> OneNote_Recy...
- 🗑 Part 1 — (Jack Attack> OneNote_Recy...

Summary

This chapter has covered the basic fundamentals of OneNote and you will have hopefully gained familiarity with the interface. Feel free to play about for a while longer to get the hang of OneNote if you'd like. You'll begin to put the features into practice in the next chapter where we begin to set up your GTD system. Later on in the book we'll cover advanced OneNote features, tips and tricks that will fine tune your productivity.

7 - SETTING UP ONENOTE FOR GTD IN 5 SAVVY STEPS

You'll need to set aside a bit of time to set up OneNote for GTD (unless you already have the GTD system in place and are just transferring your current lists over). Don't sweat though, the time you set aside initially for this will reap rewards for you long into the future.

The suggested time necessary here is at least an hour so load up OneNote when you have the time and we can get started!

Step 1: Set Up Your Notebook and Sections

The first step towards getting things done with OneNote is to create a new notebook by clicking on "File" and "New". You will want to make sure you select the "OneDrive – Personal" tab then input your new notebook name. A prompt will then appear asking you if you would like to share your notebook with other people select "Not now" (unless there are people you would like to share your notebook with).

Once you've set up your new notebook you'll be brought to the notebook page. The 7 essential sections you'll need to add are listed below:

In

Next Actions

Waiting For

Projects

Someday/Maybe

Reference

Trigger

Before you begin adding the lists as sections it will help to think ahead and decide how you would like these lists to be set up. They can be set up either as 'Sections' or as 'Section Groups' which will allow you to create further sections under the section group.

The lists I would suggest keeping as solely just 'Sections' would be In, Reference and Trigger. This isn't a hard and fast rule however I find that having too many sections can diminish efficiency, especially if the sections aren't being utilized. As a result I find that for these lists section groups aren't required. For instance, with Trigger, simply creating new pages under this section for each area you would like trigger words for will suffice (e.g. each new page can serve for

Professional, Personal, Health and so on with your trigger words written on the pages.)

With Projects, Someday/Maybe, Waiting For and Next Actions, you may want to create a section group for these lists as they will most likely house greater than 25 items under each list and as a result it makes it much easier to navigate these lists when you have seperate sections underneath the overarching section group.

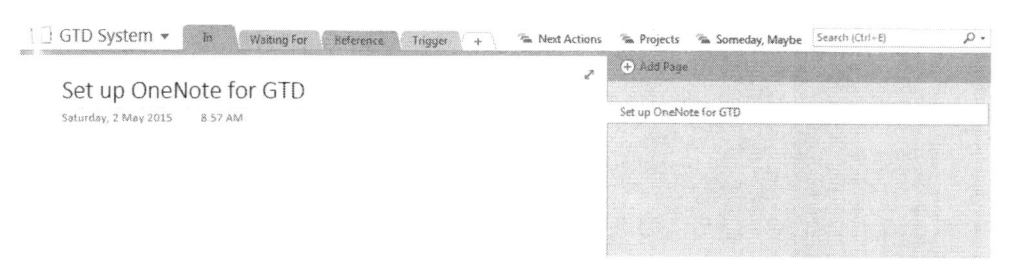

To add a section (press Ctrl + T or left click on the + sign), otherwise for a section group right click on the horizontal bar housing the sections and select "New Section Group". A new tab will appear allowing you to then input the appropriate name for the tab. If you need to re-name a tab, simply double click on it and you can then edit the name.

If you wish, you may also add an Archive section and this can serve as a section where completed projects are transferred to. You may want to archive completed projects to store information related to a project just in case you ever need to refer back to it in the future. This is particularly helpful when enquiries about a project you completed 5 months ago show up randomly. Having the Archive list allows you to easily find the relevant information and hand it over without spending countless hours trying to find the right document. If you ever need to refer back to completed projects for yourself, this also means the notes will be at arm's reach and can be retrieved with a quick search.

Setting up your sections will only take a couple of minutes but this is the basis of your entire productivity framework so take the time to make it right for you as you only have to do it once. Make sure everything is in an order that you're happy and comfortable with and please feel free to change the names of the lists to suit your preferences. If you do this, just make sure you keep the context of the lists consistent (i.e. Next Actions list should contain only next actions despite whatever you call it). A lot of people don't find "in" a very descriptive term so you could call that section "uncategorized tasks" if you like or "capture".

Don't get overly pedantic with the sections here, they can easily be edited, added or deleted as you see fit later down the track. Nothing is set in stone with GTD or OneNote which is great for adaptability and flexibility especially as you get more comfortable with them and start experimenting.

Keeping the lists separated and with hard defined edges is very important in the success of your GTD system. So ensure that your lists/sections don't start melding into one another (especially if you change their names!) as it makes the system a lot harder for you to use as you might find yourself running in circles trying to find the wrong things in the right places. Once you've set up your sections, we can start filling your "in" list which will then flow through to the rest of your lists.

Step 2: Setting Up the In List

Okay! So here's the fun part where you get to add all of the things you need to work on into your "in" list. Click on the section which represents your "in" list. You will want each task, action or idea you can think of to be on a separate page so that it's easier for you to move them into the appropriate lists later on.

In the future once this is set up, you'll be adding action items, tasks or ideas to the "in" list as soon as they arrive (or close to it) with the items to be processed once a day, or every second day to make sure your list doesn't get to excessive amounts.

As you may be starting your "in" list for the first time, it's important you get everything out of your mind and onto OneNote as you'll be processing them one by one in the next step. This will eliminate any anxious thoughts that you may have forgotten something to note down and serves as the most important thing you can do to improve your productivity immensely with this brain capacity freed up.

What are you waiting for? You can begin noting like a mad man!

Just make sure everything you could possibly think of that needs to be done or should be done is written down and out of your head. This step takes up the majority of the time required to set up GTD but is well worth it. If you do it you'll soon figure out why!

TIP: Before you start noting, make sure you utilize the shortcut **Ctrl + N** to create a new page for each note quickly.

Step 3: Processing Your "In" List

Now that you have as many things as you could possibly think of in your "in" list you might feel quite relieved despite having a long list of things that need or should get done. This is the result of knowing that everything you need to do is now in one place and you won't have to constantly be remembering them or feel as if you've forgotten something!

The first time you process your "in" list it's going to take a while as you'll be processing a long list with little to no experience in processing your list. Of course in the future this will decrease and take less time as you become more proficient in determining where your tasks need to go, specifying the next actions and as you gain more familiarity with OneNote you will start breezing through your "in" list. Also, as you will be processing your list once a day, or every other day it won't overflow with items and will be easily managed.

Please note that getting "in" to empty doesn't mean you actually do all the actions you've captured. It just means identifying and acknowledging each item then deciding what it is, what it means and what you're going to do with it. When you begin processing your list feel free to refer back to the image below and use it as a guideline:

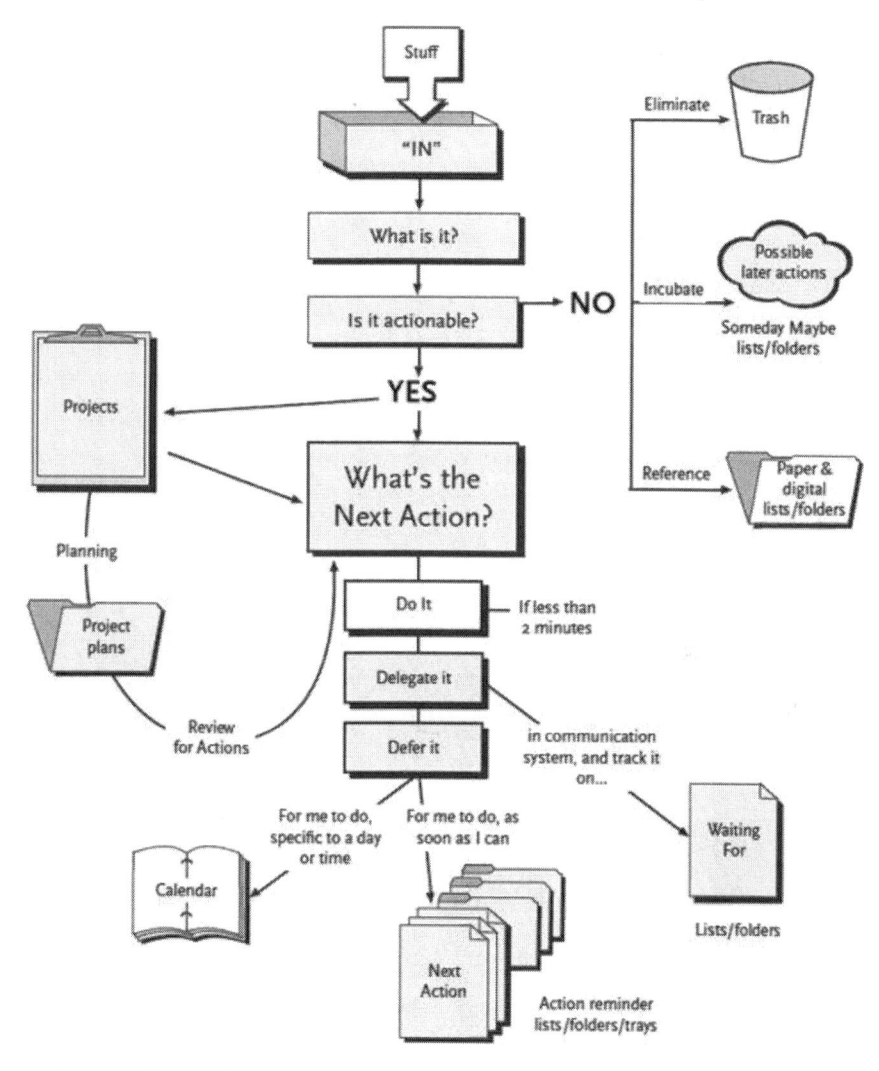

As you have the "IN" component, you must now determine for each note whether it's actionable, if it isn't then you delete (trash) it, place it into the Someday/Maybe list or put it into your Reference list for future use.

If there is an actionable task associated to it then you need to clearly specify what the next action will be. You can do this by editing the page title (Ctrl + Shift + T or clicking on it manually) to define the action as a clear, specific and visible action.

Once this is done, move on to triple D. Is it something that can be done in 2 minutes or less? If so, DO IT! Once you finish it, click on the Note and press the Delete key to trash it otherwise move it to the Archives list.

If it isn't doable in 2 minutes, you have to determine whether you want to delegate or defer it. If you're delegating it you'll need to send it to the person you're delegating the task to then move the note into the Waiting For list. You can determine whether you should be delegating or doing the task by asking yourself if you are the most appropriate person to be doing the task. Make sure you take into account the possibility of leveraging your time, even if you're capable of doing the task would it perhaps be wiser to get your assistant to undertake the task?

If you choose to defer it then you must determine if it's something that can be done whenever it's possible (i.e. has a deadline far in the future) or if it is to be done at a later date which is fixed (i.e. credit card payment due on the last day of the month or quarterly report due on the last day of the month). If it only needs to be done whenever it's possible to do so, move it to your Next Actions list.

Otherwise put it into your calendar as a MUST to be accomplished on that specific date and/or time it must be done by.

When you have determined the right course of action for the task, all you have to do now is move it to the appropriate list in OneNote. To do this you can either right click on the page title on the right hand side of the page, click "**Move or Copy**" and a box will pop up with the different sections that you can move the page to. You will then have to find the section you want the page to go, highlight that section and then click move to put it in there. I suggest getting familiar with the shortcuts and using them now (especially since you'll be using them a lot with this long "in" list") so press **Ctrl + Alt + M** to bring up the "**Move or Copy**" box instead of manually clicking each note as you process them.

Setting Up OneNote for GTD in 5 Savvy Steps

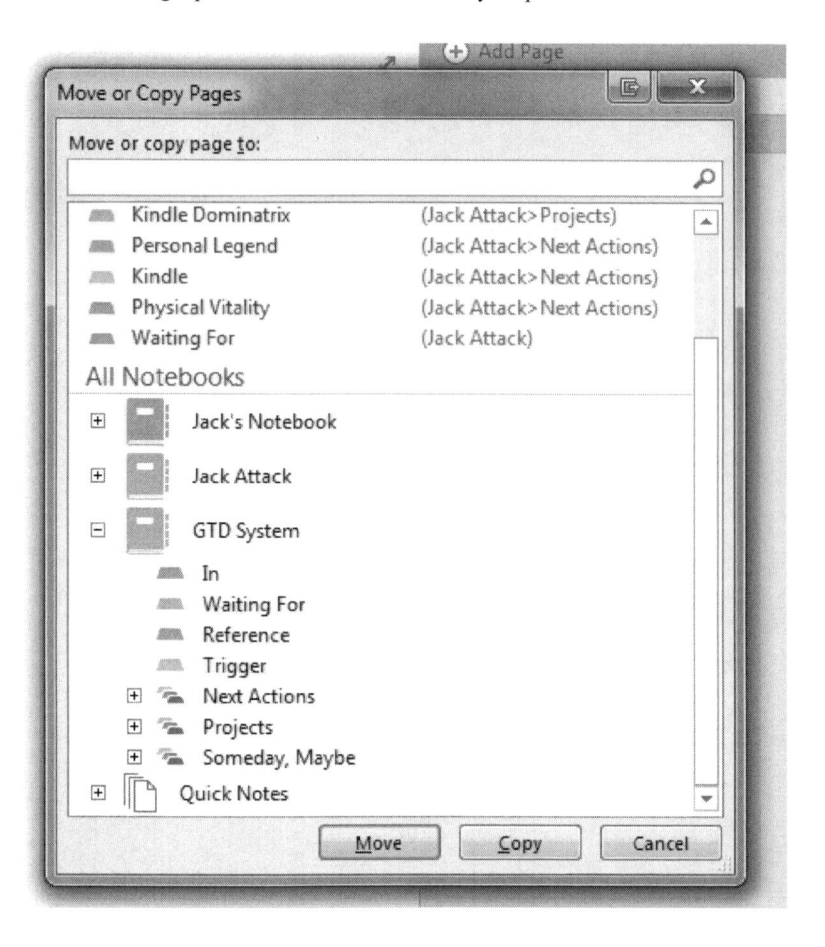

TIP: Three fundamental rules to follow when processing your "in" list.

1. Process the top item first.

2. Process one item at a time. (The only exception to this is if you find that you need to shift your focus away for at least a minute in order to make a decision about

the item – if so take 2 items at a time and never avoid any decision for longer than a minute or two.)

3. Never put anything back into "in".

If you're wondering why 2 minutes is the determinant to doing an action straight away as opposed to say a 5 minute rule then here's your answer! 2 minutes is more or less the point at which it starts taking longer to store, track and process the item than to deal with it the first time that it's in your face. In other words, it's the efficiency cutoff time, if it isn't important enough to be done, trash it. If it is, and if you're going to do it sometime soon, then now is the best time as the efficiency factor comes into play. Just make sure you're not overestimating how long 2 minutes actually is, it might help to time some of these actions as you begin to gain better judgement in this area.

Step 4: Adding Contexts

Adding contexts to your tasks is very important and makes life so much easier. Once your "in" list has been processed, you can now work through each section to add the context for each actionable item.

Imagine you're sitting on a train with your laptop out and you want to make use of the idle time on your journey by knocking out a couple of next actions. You bring up your next actions list and instead of having to wade through all of the actions (which at times may be in excess of 40) and having to determine the context required to complete each item such as needing to be in the office, or requiring certain equipment/software that you don't have with you. You'll already have contexts labelled next to each action so that you can easily skim the list and find the ones which are labelled 'laptop', and quickly determine which of these actions you should get started on.

Click on the 'Home' tab at the top (if it isn't showing already) and you should see a 'Tags' section on the right hand side of the features under 'Home'. Click on the down arrow button that has a horizontal line above it that is found next to the listed tags.

A list of tags will then appear, at the bottom of the list there will be an option to "Customize Tags", click on that and you will then be given the option to modify or add new tags. These tags will now serve as your contexts.

OneNote Ultimate User Guide to Getting Things Done

Tags

- ☑ @Computer (Ctrl+1)
- ⭐ @Skype (Ctrl+2)
- ? @Anywhere (Ctrl+3)
- @Phone (Ctrl+4)
- Definition (Ctrl+5)
- ✎ Highlight (Ctrl+6)
- Contact (Ctrl+7)
- 🏠 Address (Ctrl+8)
- 📞 Phone number (Ctrl+
- 🌐 Web site to visit
- 💡 Idea
- 🔒 Password
- ! Critical
- Project A
- Project B
- 🎬 Movie to see
- 📖 Book to read
- ♪ Music to listen to
- 🌐 Source for article
- 💬 Remember for blog
- Discuss with <Person
- Discuss with <Person
- Discuss with manage
- Send in email
- Schedule meeting
- Call back
- To Do priority 1
- To Do priority 2
- Client request
- Customize Tags...
- Remove Tag

Setting Up OneNote for GTD in 5 Savvy Steps

You should modify the tags to things which you know will be commonly used as contexts (such as "@computer", "@desk", "@laptop" or "@phone") and you can slowly adapt, edit and add the contexts which aren't as common later on when they start showing up.

Choose a tag icon that allows you to add a checkbox and this will now serve as your context.

Make sure you modify the tags which already have shortcuts assigned to them, these tags with shortcuts assigned will have the shortcuts shown next to them such as (Ctrl + 1) or (Ctrl + 2). Once you've modified them, all you need to do is click on the page of your next action note and press the shortcut key (Ctrl + number) to tag this next action under the right context. When you've done that, an empty square box will show up that you'll be able to tick once you've finished the action.

By providing these contexts it streamlines your ability to find tasks that you're able to carry out in any environment you happen to find yourself in. From here, all you'll need to do is click "Find Tags" at the top of the screen and click the drop down box "Group tags by" and then choose the "Tag Name". If you tick the "Show Only Unchecked Items", you'll have a list of all of your next actions that need to get done which are separated by their contexts. This way you can scan through the list for the context that suits you, which is much easier than wading through all of your notes and having to determine the context of each one!

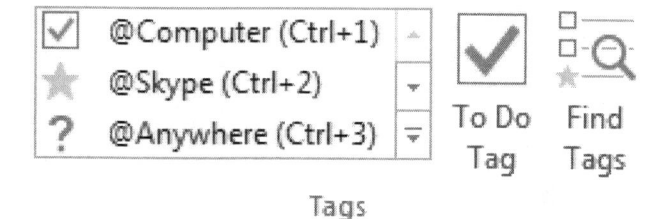

Tags

To Do Tag

Find Tags

> **Tags Summary**
>
> Search completed
>
> Group tags by:
>
> [Tag name ▼]
>
> ☐ Show only unchecked items
>
> **@Computer**
> ☐ Brainstorm new header for website
> ☐ Update excel budget sheet
>
> **@Phone**
> Call accountant for tax implications on ...

Once you've completed the task just check the box and viola it's removed from your list!

Step 5: Link Up With Outlook

A lot of people communicate by e-mail these days (this could be the understatement of the year) so integrating with outlook is useful for two purposes – firstly, you can easily delegate by emailing relevant notes to a colleague and, secondly, you can import anything you need into your "in" list.

As any software developed by Microsoft will automatically ask you to login using your Microsoft account they too will also automatically be linked together. The easiest way to use Outlook with OneNote is to simply click the "Send to OneNote" button in Outlook that will transfer e-mails into any section of your notebooks. The content of the email, subject, sender, recipient and text from the email will transfer over. This button can be found in the Move section of the Outlook ribbon.

In OneNote, under the 'Home' tab, on the far right there is an 'Email page' button under the Outlook ribbon. Clicking this button will turn the contents of the OneNote page you are currently on into a new email message. All you're required to do from here is simply input the subject and recipient and you can then send your notes off.

If you go back to the Outlook section of OneNote under the 'Home' tab you can find several extra options. One of the options is "meeting details" - this will show you a list of today's meetings imported from your Outlook calendar. You also have the option of creating a task from a note that will go straight into your Outlook calendar. You can do this by clicking "Outlook Tasks" and setting the date and time for a reminder of when you want the task done by.

Summary

You now have your GTD notebook set up in OneNote and you're ready to start putting your GTD system into action. Before you move onto the next chapter make sure you have your GTD system set up and your "next tasks" ready to complete. In the next chapter we're going to use the GTD system and put it all into practice!

8 - GTD & ONENOTE IN TANDEM

Now you have your system set up you can start using your system and you will begin to notice a significant improvement in your productivity. The most important thing you have to do to ensure the system works (and sticks!) is to get into the routine of utilizing the system, because even if you have the best software and the best system on hand – if you aren't using it, it won't do jack for you.

Following this routine will take you from an unorganized mess into a productivity ninja!

Step 1: Filling Your "In" List

Add to your "in" list whenever you receive something, as soon as practicable put it into your "in" list. They don't have to be actual tasks, as long as the thought pops into your mind continuously then you need to note it down, this way you can clear your mind from the thought and operate from a "mind like water". Put everything into your "in" list and clear the useless things out later when you process your list.

You don't need to make everything in your "in" list perfectly worded, as long as it has the information you need to trigger the thought that sparked the idea, it gets the job done. For example, you can simply copy and paste some text from an article if that reminds you of what needs to be done (either to read the article or implement the marketing strategy outlined in the article) or take a snapshot if you like and get it into your "in" list, you can turn it into a succinctly worded task if you need to later on when it's processed. Feel free to use as many abbreviations and acronyms as you require – as long as it gets the message across when you later process the note.

Step 2: Processing Your "In" List

Take the time every day to process your list, I highly recommend doing this at the end of the day so you can empty your list. That way you start the next day with an empty "in" list and a full list of "Next Actions" to work on. However, it's fine to choose any other time of the day – do what works best for you, but I recommend setting a specific time of the day to do it and make it a habit. At a minimum you should process your "in" list every two days otherwise it will start building up and you may get paralysis by analysis from the thought of having to process all the ideas or tasks that are listed.

When you're processing your list, go through each item of your "in" list one by one and make sure you take the time to turn any "next actions" into physical, actionable tasks and place the others in their appropriate lists such as someday/maybe and reference, otherwise please trash it. By taking a bit of extra time now to do this, you save a tremendous amount of time later on. Also don't forget triple D, do it if it falls under the 2 minute rule, delegate it otherwise defer it. To reiterate, the 2 minute rule is an arbitrary figure, you can increase or decrease this time limit depending on how much time, energy and focus you have available to process your list.

Step 3: Always Do Your Weekly Review

Your weekly review needs to be performed weekly (which is why it's not called a "whenever you like" review). Set a specific day and time each week to review your lists, and take the time to do it properly. Not reviewing properly is as bad as not reviewing at all. As you can access OneNote from practically any device – you have no excuse not to be on top of your reviews! Make it fun, put on your favorite music and get jiggy with it, none of these steps need to be mundane or boring! Do whatever it takes to make the process fun and exciting and come to it with an abundance of energy and you'll find you'll start looking forward to the process and get it done in less and less time (as you get more and more done each week!).

By doing a weekly review you ensure that you'll always be on top of your workload. You make sure that you don't have too little or too much work in your next actions and that you're always moving towards your end goals and outcomes with your projects.

Weekly reviews are one of the most important steps in the system,

DO NOT skip it!!

Step 4: Outlook is Your Friend

You want to utilize the integration between Outlook and OneNote to its fullest potential. This is one of the greatest benefits of having software with cross-compatibility.

You can start by transferring any e-mails you need to into OneNote, which saves you time from having to copy and paste things across. It's up to you as to how you transfer the e-mails across, I'd recommend transferring them across to your "in" list whenever you read them, or you could treat your emails like an "in" list and process them before transferring them into the section they need to be in at the end of each day.

The other way you can use Outlook to increase productivity is to use it for delegating tasks. By simply clicking the "E-Mail Page" button you can easily delegate a task without needing to make a call or drafting up a detailed message. By doing it in this manner, you will have a copy in OneNote of exactly what you sent to the person carrying out the task, which makes things easier if they have questions or when you need to chase things up closer to the due date.

Step 5: Add a Separate Page for Everything

You may be tempted to add your notes to an existing page on OneNote because it saves a bit of time, especially if the notes are slightly related. Restrain yourself from doing so! By having notes on separate pages it makes it easier to find them when you need to refer to them at a later date, it also makes it easier to email the notes when you need to. Apart from the other benefits, this will also make your notes tidier. It only takes a few seconds to add a new page, but if you're searching high and low through OneNote to find that one page holding the notes you need – you'll wish you'd taken those extra seconds to simply open up a new page!

Step 6: Don't Limit Yourself To Just Typing Notes

Limiting yourself to just typing notes in your "in" list makes things harder for you. Firstly, it limits your ability to capture notes, especially when you just don't have the time to type a note out. This limits your productivity as the note will then linger in your mind like an unwanted guest and diminish your focus. Secondly, it may not be the best option to type the information as a note as it could be quicker to take a picture and upload it. Thirdly, you may not capture the full scale or idea of your note in text format that could only be done so in visual or audio format.

Make use of every possible way you can get the note down. If typing the note is the best way then use that method. But on the other hand if an image can get the message across better, use an image. If you find it easier to speak then use an audio note, or if you can actually record the original message (i.e. if you have a voice mail you need to respond to on your mobile), then record it. Make use of all of the mediums that you can to take your notes down, this way you won't have any open loops in your head and you can focus solely on the task at hand.

Summary

By following this structure, you will develop consistency and efficiency in the way you run your GTD system. Consistency is critical in ensuring you get more organized and optimize productivity as it will make sure you don't slip back to your old habits and life of chaos!

"We are what we repeatedly do. Excellence, then, is not an act, but a habit."

-Aristotle

9 - 6 PRODUCTIVITY HACKS & TRICKS WITH ONENOTE

You've got the basics of OneNote down and you've now set up your GTD system which is up and running – great job! Now it's time to pick up a few extra tips and tricks for OneNote that'll save you time over the long run.

Copying Text from Images

As detailed earlier, OneNote has the ability to search images for text displayed on them, which is possible thanks to its optical character recognition (OCR). The OCR in OneNote is so powerful that, as well as being able to search through text in images, you're also able to copy the text straight from the images (including handwritten text) with minimal errors.

The ability to copy text from images opens up a ton of possibilities for GTD. For example, if you have a note left on your desk for something you need to do, you can snap a photo of it on your tablet – put it in OneNote and then copy the text from the image so that you can edit it into an actionable task when you want to put it in your next actions list.

If there are going to be a lot of situations where you won't have access to a computer, or your work doesn't utilize computers often, then this is something you will want to make high use of. To copy the text all you have to do is right click on the image and select '**Copy Text from Picture**' then hit Ctrl + V to paste the text.

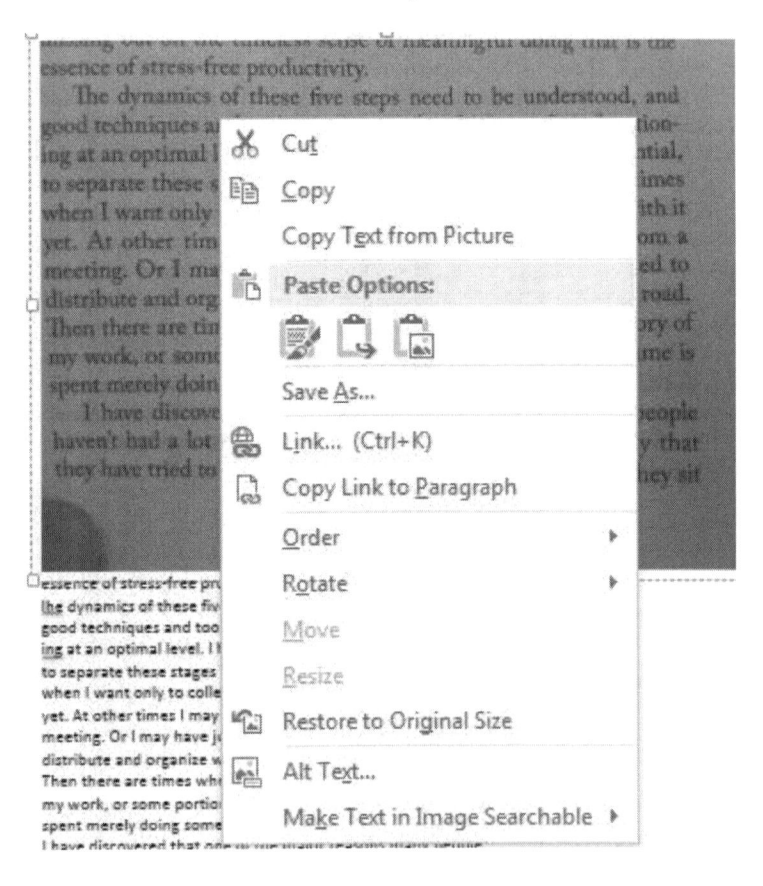

Using OneNote When OneNote Isn't Open

You've already been told about the **Win+ S** shortcut to take a screenshot, which you can use when OneNote isn't open. But there are even more shortcuts you can still use when OneNote isn't open.

Win + N will open up a quick note for you to note down anything you need to note. This is useful when you're in the middle of doing some work and you receive information that you need to quickly add to your "in" list. **Win + Shift + N** is a nifty shortcut to open OneNote whenever you need to (even if it isn't currently open).

Edit Your Notes Faster

There are a lot of different shortcuts you can use inside of OneNote. These shortcuts can be used to edit and format your notes swiftly and easily. Below are a number of common shortcuts for you to use, if you want the full list of shortcuts, you can see them on the Microsoft website by [clicking here](). I highly recommend going through the list and testing ones which stand out for you to find out which ones you could use often to become even more efficient with OneNote. If you happen to find some (and I'm sure you will if you go through them), create your own cheat sheet and print it out for quick reference until you memorize them.

Some of the most common and useful shortcuts I use are:

Control + 1 to start a checklist

Control + 2 for a star/custom tag

Control + Shift + 1 for an Outlook reminder

Control + . (period) to start a bullet point list

Control + K to insert a link

Control + N to add a new page at the end of the section

Control + M opens a new OneNote window when you need to work with multiple sections and pages.

Control + Y to undo the last action.

Control + Y to redo the last action.

These shortcuts allow you to quickly edit and format your notes, by making use of them you will easily become more efficient. You may only save a few seconds from utilizing these shortcuts each time, but over the long haul this adds up to a significant amount of time.

Access OneNote from Your Mobile Home Screen

If you use an Android phone (or tablet) you can pin notebooks or pages onto your home screen. Being able to access your workbooks from your home screen will make it quicker and easier for you to access notebooks or pages.

To add OneNote to your home screen on Android, all you'll need to do is choose the option from the top menu of the OneNote Android app and pin the page or notebook to your home screen.

To place a widget on your home screen, hold your finger down where there is open space on your home screen, then click "Apps and Widgets" and choose the OneNote widget.

Search Audio and Video Files

You can actually set up OneNote to search through your audio and video files just like you can with text and images. This makes it easier for you to find these files when you need them, this can be important if you find it easier to take audio notes rather than text notes. I lived through the frustration of having a full playlist of audio clips with no way of searching for the one sentence I required to progress on a project in my past life. This feature on OneNote is definitely a lifesaver, literally!

You can enable this option for searching audio and video files by clicking **File → Options** then going to the **Audio & Video** tab. Once there, check the box next to "**Enable searching audio and video recordings for words**". If you're going to be using audio and video notes on a regular basis then I urge you to enable this option.

Doing Math Calculations in OneNote

If you need to do simple calculations, forget about your calculator app or physical calculator! Just type the math equation anywhere on OneNote's page surface, followed by the equal sign then press the spacebar or Enter and OneNote will perform the calculation. For example, you can do simple calculations such as "5999/32" by typing "5999/32 =" or "5+20+45+50=" and OneNote will do these calculations for you.

Summary

There are many features in OneNote, the best of which have been shown in this book. Now that you have this productivity system in your arsenal you'll be able to get things done easily, quickly and unbelievably efficiently with a "mind like water", minimizing your overall stress levels and leaving you feeling better than you've ever felt before!

10 - YOU'VE WON!

Congratulations on reaching the end of this book! I trust that you'll start getting things done in a much more organized and productive fashion than you have been in the past.

Now that you've worked your way through the book your mission is to keep on top of OneNote and your GTD system. Make sure you don't skip the time you need to process your "in" list at the chosen time of the day you have set to process it and certainly never, ever skip your weekly reviews (I'll be watching!).

By sticking rigidly to the GTD system you'll bring a consistency to your work to levels that you've never experienced. You'll be more organized, more productive and demolish any task that comes your way.

The system you need to keep to isn't simply the actual GTD system but the system of how you use OneNote as well. If you keep to a simple, consistent way of taking down notes for your "in" box then you'll find that your consistency makes the system become an ingrained habit, rather than something you need to consciously think about doing. By doing this you will start to ensure you capture all relevant information that you need to and will increase your chances of operating from a state with zero to minimal open loops.

If you've gotten through the book and you haven't started putting anything into action then hop on your computer, go back through the book and start setting up OneNote. While it's nice to simply know the information – it's significantly better to have a working productivity system which you can use to keep yourself organized and get stuff done!

Enjoy your extra time and dedicate it to other tasks that bring greater balance into your life, start doing more of the things you know you should be doing but maybe haven't been such as spending more time with your children, maintaining your health or even better, doing your taxes.

What's great about this system is that the more you use it, the more productive and organized you'll become. So, if you think you're organized now – wait and see how organized you feel two weeks from now and you'll be blown away by the changes.

Finally, thank you for reading the book, and I hope you continue to reap the rewards of putting these steps into action!

If you found this book helpful at all, it would be a huge favor if you could leave a review for this book on Amazon providing your honest feedback. It'd be greatly appreciated and this way we can reach out to more people and help everyone learn to become productivity ninjas!

To leave a review type in the link below to a web browser:

http://amzn.to/1EJR45O

Thank you and best of luck, go start getting things done!

11 - FREE BONUS!

As a thank you for reading my guide I would love to share with you a free bonus – 5 Unknown Productivity Tools!

Please access your free bonus by typing in the link below into a web browser.

<u>http://bit.ly/1DOFcvm</u>

More Resources

Getting Things Done: The Art of Stress-Free Productivity (2015) by David Allen

Flow: The Psychology of Optimal Experience by Mihaly Csikszentmihalyi

The Rise of Superman: Decoding the Science of Ultimate Human Performance by Steven Kotler

INDEX

"

"in" list 9, 10, 12, 13, 17, 22, 33, 36, 53, 54, 57, 58, 59, 64, 67, 68, 70, 71, 75, 79

2

2 minute rule 12, 69

C

calendar......................10, 20, 21, 57, 65
capture 9, 19, 35, 36, 46, 52, 71, 80
context .. 7, 9, 14, 19, 52, 59, 60, 62, 63

D

David Allen 4, 5, 7, 83
defer 12, 56, 69
delegate......... 12, 21, 34, 56, 64, 69, 70

E

Evernote ....iv, 25, 27, 28, 29, 30, 31, 32

F

flow................................6, 8, 35, 53

G

Getting Things Done ....i, iv, 1, 3, 4, 5, 7, 83
GTD .. iv, 2, 3, 5, 6, 7, 8, 9, 10, 15, 20, 23, 26, 33, 35, 39, 47, 49, 52, 53, 66, 67, 72, 73, 79
goals 6, 69
guide................................1, 2, 4, 82

K

karate 7

M

memory 8
mental clarity...................................... 8
Microsoft Office................................ 25
Mihaly Csikszentmihalyi 6, 83
mind like water................ 6, 7, 8, 67, 78

N

next actions 9, 11, 14, 15, 20, 22, 34, 52, 54, 59, 63, 68, 69, 74
Next Actions . 12, 13, 14, 19, 20, 22, 34, 43, 50, 51, 52, 56, 68

O

objectives 9
OneDrive..........................25, 40, 42, 49
OneNote .... i, ii, iv, 1, 2, 3, 9, 15, 20, 23, 25, 26, 27, 28, 29, 30, 31, 32, 33, 34, 35, 36, 39, 40, 41, 45, 46, 47, 49, 52, 53, 54, 57, 64, 65, 66, 67, 69, 70, 73, 74, 75, 76, 77, 78, 79, 80
open loops 10, 16, 72, 80
outcome 11, 12, 13, 14, 15
overwhelmed 8

P

physical action 12, 13, 14
principle... 6
priorities 6
problems 1, 7
processing...... 10, 13, 53, 54, 55, 58, 68
    processed 10, 53, 59, 68

productivity.....1, 2, 5, 7, 14, 26, 31, 33, 34, 47, 52, 53, 67, 70, 71, 72, 78, 80, 81
project....................... 15, 16, 17, 51, 77
projects 1, 15, 16, 17, 18, 21, 22, 23, 43, 51, 52, 69
Projects 15, 16, 18, 19, 43, 50, 51
psyche 8, 13

R

reference list 11, 22
Reference List 21
Roy Baumeister 8

S

someday/maybe list.................... 11, 22
Stephen Kotler 6
stress.. 2, 5, 78
system... 1, 2, 3, 4, 5, 6, 8, 9, 10, 13, 16, 20, 22, 23, 26, 28, 33, 35, 47, 49, 52, 66, 67, 69, 72, 73, 78, 79, 80

T

tasks .. 7, 8, 9, 10, 20, 33, 34, 36, 52, 53, 54, 59, 63, 66, 67, 68, 70, 80
tension 2
Trigger word....................................... 18

V

vision.. ii

W

Waiting For 15, 43, 50, 51, 56
Weekly Review 21, 69
work 2, 5, 6, 8, 15, 20, 21, 22, 26, 30, 31, 32, 34, 35, 40, 43, 53, 59, 68, 69, 74, 75, 76, 79

Z

zone 6

Made in the USA
Middletown, DE
13 August 2015